My Mom was
MURDERED

A Survival Story

An experienced counselor shares her personal journey
through the devastation of a violent crime in hope that
her survival techniques will help other victims.

My Mom was MURDERED

PAMALA MESSINGER

authorHOUSE®

AuthorHouse™ LLC
1663 Liberty Drive
Bloomington, IN 47403
www.authorhouse.com
Phone: 1-800-839-8640

Published by AuthorHouse   04/11/2014

ISBN: 978-1-4969-0287-0 (sc)
ISBN: 978-1-4969-0285-6 (hc)
ISBN: 978-1-4969-0286-3 (e)

Library of Congress Control Number: 2014906513

Contents

Dedication

I dedicate this book to my husband George, who has supported me throughout our thirty two year journey. Also, I must give love and thanks to my very creative children, Megan, AJ, and Joshua. Their antics have made my writing a joy. Of course I can't forget my bonus daughter, Lorah. (We discovered each other about 14 years ago and she has added spice to our family.)

My heart has a special place for my friends whom have shared their life with me—yes Barbara—I am including you too! Finally, I would like to thank my sisters and brother for their unconditional support and love. My life has been enriched by all of you.

Foreword

Through my years of education and counseling, I have become quite familiar with the stages of grief first introduced by Elisabeth Kubler-Ross. In fact, I remember making a study of it in one of my counseling classes. I have helped numerous clients, students, and friends through the tumultuous stages of death, and personally experienced and survived its devastation. I guess you could have said I was an expert of sorts in the field of grief. Then, on the day of Cinco de Mayo, 1992, my mother was murdered. Any heretofore knowledge I might have claimed flew out the window, and I was left to fend for myself.

I remember the day it happened. I worked in a largely Hispanic school, so most of the classrooms were filled with celebrations for Mexico's Independence. Though I participated, I had this nagging feeling of something not quite right, like the universe was slightly off center. I kept thinking my spiritual antenna was sending signals of impending disaster, but what it was I could not identify. It seemed like I was participating in a fog of dreadful anticipation that day. My friends later told me that I had talked about my mother constantly throughout the day. Was this a form of precognition? I don't know, but it certainly could have been.

This is my story and the stages of grief I went through. _My Mother was Murdered_, is filled with personal experiences for each stage of my grief and paired with specific information and techniques that can be used with each stage.

As with all types of deaths, I don't begin to understand what each of you are going through. It is my hope, however, that you will find some peace and understanding in my words and your journey will make a little more sense to you. Though I have a Master of Science Degree in Counseling and 30 years of experience, I don't pretend to be an expert in grief therapy for murder victims. I am but a fellow victim who seeks to help other victims.

"Space for your personal thoughts"

Chapter 1

SHOCK, DISBELIEF, AND DENIAL

It was around 2:30 pm when a colleague came to my classroom door and whispered that I needed to go to the front office. I remember grabbing her arm and asking, "What's wrong?"

"It's only a phone call," she said, "I will watch your class."

Thoughts of what it could be flew through my head, while I slowly moved toward the front office. My feet felt like I was moving through molasses. Then another teacher asked me, "Why are you crying?"

I touched my face in amazement; unaware that I was indeed crying.

"I don't know," I remember answering, "but, something is really wrong."

I was almost incoherent when I answered the phone, and my sister Cindy said, "Oh, you already know."

"No," I said, "but it is something terrible. Just tell me quickly."

In her very gentle way, she told me mom and Christine, her lesbian partner, had been shot while stabilizing a fence post on the farm property where we grew up. Our sometimes friendly, sometimes crabby neighbor, James Brooks, shot them. They were dead.

Immediately my legs collapsed and I fell to the floor moving my head back and forth, physically denying what I was hearing. Someone was screaming hysterically, and in some remote corner of my mind I knew it was me.

I could faintly hear my sister whispering, "Breathe, Pam, breathe."

But I couldn't. In order to survive that precise moment, I entered the black void of unconsciousness. I remember at one point my sister Linda called and I told her I couldn't understand what she was saying and she said, "They are dead. Mom and Christine are dead."

At that point I simply could not process that information. I threw the phone against the wall trying to get it away from me, scooted as far away as I could, and fell into unconsciousness again. During this timeless moment I saw and felt many really weird experiences. I could hear screaming. It seemed like thousands and thousands of women were screaming. I felt connected to them and felt their pain as I could not feel mine. I wanted to raise my head and scream with them, until our joined voices could be heard in the neither world of injustice and hurt; our spirits united in one swirling mass of raging power, but some part of me knew that if I did, I wouldn't be able to stop.

Time slipped away without my knowledge. I could not fight my way back to consciousness. At some point, after what I think was hours of the school nurse trying to bring me back with smelling salts, I was transported by ambulance to a nearby hospital. This was an ending and beginning for me. I was never the same after that.

I remember being released from the hospital and the doctor wanting to know if there was anything he could do. "Turn back the clock," I whispered. Somehow I made it to the car and from there we went to a travel agent. I remember sitting there crying while she frantically worked trying to get me on a flight. The next thing I knew, I was in bed. My children's nanny brought me in some orange juice. I don't remember what I did with it. The calls kept coming. I answered some, and found I couldn't talk. There was just blank silence in answer to their questions. I wouldn't accept what people were saying. "Leave me alone with my thoughts," I remember wishing.

"Get them to stop saying mom is dead," I said to my husband George.

There were long blank spaces where sometimes it was quiet, and sometimes I heard women screaming. I don't really know what happened next except that somehow I was on a plane looking out the window. I must have cried because no one talked to me on the whole trip—not even to offer me food. At least I don't think they did. I wrote a poem for my mother at one point, then stared out the window some more.

We hear the silence of our soul
For a piece of it is gone
No longer will we feel
Your solid support
Goodbye dear mother
Brown eyes with tears
Goodbye

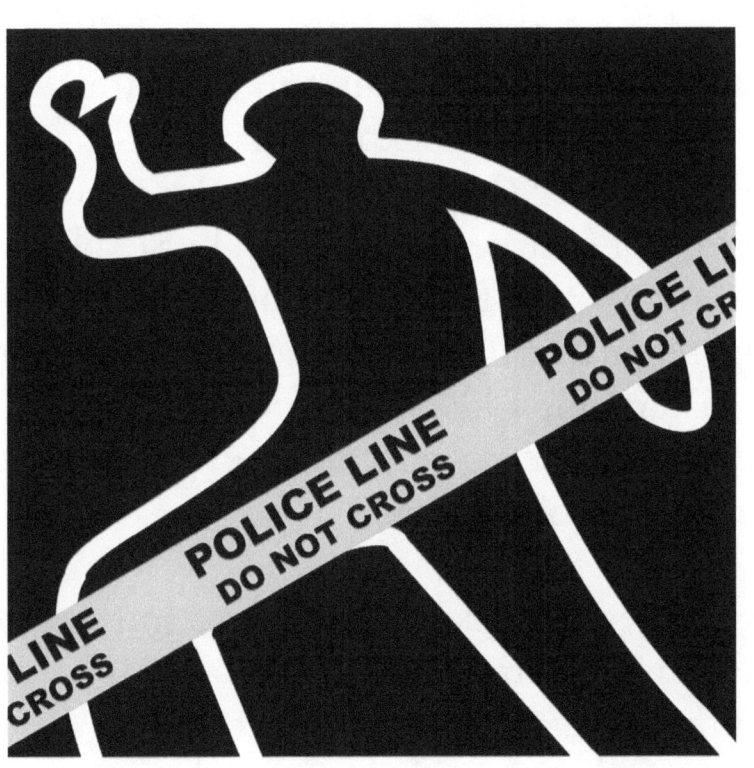

When someone is murdered, the family is often sent on an emotional rollercoaster where they experience wave after wave of anger, guilt, blame, depression and denial. Since the death is sudden and so traumatic it throws the family right into the middle of these emotions and adds to the intensity of grief. It is not uncommon to blank out and lose time. Many victims of violence experience post-traumatic stress disorder (PTSD) within the first couple of years of a loved one's death. Large blocks of time are missing from the subconscious in both long term memory and short term memory. My sister Linda blocks out huge pieces of her childhood due to a combination of spousal abuse and mom's murder.

Like an earthquake, murder victims seem to share these moments of aftershock. It happens in funny little ways; such as, dazed looks, fainting spells, sentences never completed. Some people get anxiety attacks, and still others physically react by real or imagined heart attacks. It is really important that you drink a lot of water during this time. Friends will try to get you to eat, and that's great if you can, but if that is impossible you might ask them to bring you some water. This gives your friends something to make them feel useful and it replenishes the fluids you will be losing.

Post-Traumatic Stress Disorder

Post-traumatic Stress Disorder (PTSD) is a high stress syndrome that follows a psychologically traumatic event. We usually associate PTSD with war veterans. In fact, I first remember hearing the disorder called Shell Shock. However, we are seeing more and more victims of violent crimes develop many of the same symptoms. When I was trying to understand what was happening to me, I ran across a description by Richard W. Cress (2005) in his book, <u>The Value of a Smile: Victimization 101</u>. His description really resonated within me.

He explained that the circumstances of violent crimes are outside of the usual emotions we go through during the more common life experiences; such as death, chronic illness, divorce, or invasive life changes. Like me, he had experienced other forms of grief, which come with their own set of issues. He also recognized the complications that occur when the death is violent as being more invasive and harder to muddle through.

It is important to note that as individuals our reactions will differ from each other. Our symptoms might begin immediately or appear much later. They might last for years, months, or even reappear when we least expect it. Everyone's experience will be as unique as we are as individuals. It is my belief that most victims will suffer some form of PTSD, and would benefit from recognizing the symptoms.

In his book, Richard W. Cress listed symptoms that I really liked, so I am including the list found in his book, with some minor changes to reflect my personal story.

Common Symptoms:

1. **Sleep problems**; such as difficulty falling asleep and or nightmares, in which the traumatic event is relived.
2. **Anger** can be directed or broadly based. Anger that is focused, however, can be a mechanism that delays the onset of the disorder. Over the years, I now believe

that directed anger, if controlled, can be a healthy, healing mechanism."

3. **Depression** is a deep sadness at the loss often accompanied by hopelessness of the occasion. Depression results from an emptiness in your life that can't be filled.

4. **Withdrawn** from family members, close friends and prior activities. It becomes just too difficult to talk about everyday occurrences. My faith in the goodness of human nature was gone.

5. **Guilt feelings** can take the form of survival guilt. For example, I remember thinking that if I had been home to pick up the phone when my mother called me she would never have been outside where she was murdered. I discovered her voice on my voice mail after she died. She was calling me before she went out to confront the gunman.

6. **Becoming Hypercritical** of authority systems such as the government or criminal justice system for their lack of sensitivity, responsiveness or effectiveness. Boy, did I feel this emotion! Especially, with the police who seemed to have no feelings at all. In retrospect, I believe they were just doing their jobs to the best of their abilities.

7. **Emotional Insulation** where the individual loses the ability to receive or give love.
8. **Alcohol or Drug Abuse** is used in attempt to block the pain. Of course, it doesn't work and potentially causes more problems.
9. **Flashbacks** or a reliving of the event. Often the flashbacks are in slow motion. In my case, I can recall exactly the events leading up to actual hearing of my mother's murder; I can minutely recall the overwhelming emotions I experienced.
10. **Anniversary Anxiety** where increased emotional problems occur during the approaching anniversary of the trauma. To this day, I don't like to acknowledge Cinco De Mayo Day, because I was celebrating this event when I found out about my mom. For about five years after the murder, I was very fragile on May 5th. Twenty two years later, I still complete my yearly ritual of burning a candle, sharing mom stories with my children, and saying a prayer for others experiencing tragedy.
11. **Phobias or Fears** which can significantly affect the freedom of movement or even occupation of the individual.

12. **Complaints of Impaired Memory or problems with concentration** where both long term and short term memories are altered significantly.

13. **Unpredictable or Explosive behavior with minimal or no obvious provocation** where behavioral control is lost. I believe I was okay here; but my husband may have a different memory! Seriously, I think all of my siblings and I suffered from this to one degree or another.

14. **Impulsive behavior**, such as sudden trips or changes in lifestyle.

I strongly recommend that a victim experiencing any of the above symptoms that disrupt the individual's life style should seek treatment from a practitioner experienced in treating this disorder. Often it is not enough to write about feelings and events of the trauma situation immediately following the trauma. I was able to maintain my sanity by writing, but it would have been so much easier with professional help. At the time there was so little known about victims of murder. Most of my family has been trained in helping professions and I remember us talking to each other for hours at a time, many times a week. This helped more than I can express with words.

"Space for your personal thoughts"

Chapter 2

ZOMBIE FUNCTIONING

I walked zombie like off the plane where two longtime friends picked me up—Paula and Pamela. When I saw them my legs gave out and I started crying harder. I don't know why. They held me up and we walked to the car. They were talking, but I didn't really hear them. I was just glad they were there. They were trying to prepare me for what I would see when I got to my old farm house, but my mind refused to process the information. When we pulled up to the house, there were TV cameras parked across the street. I saw the yellow police tape and bodies outlined in white on the ground at the end of the circle drive. That is it. I fainted, but came to as my brother carried me inside. I truly don't know what happened then. I remember thinking why is this happening? I am always calm and strong during a storm, but not this time. At some point, I worried about my friends, "where did they go?"

"When did they leave?"

Until this day, I don't know what happened. My four siblings and I did a lot of hugging and crying, I remember that.

At one point, I sat on the porch with my childhood friend Mary. I know we talked about really important subjects, but I have no memory of what we were talking about.

The next day I walked with my sister Cindy to the place where mom had fallen. Her body outlined in white paint marked where she had fallen on her back with her legs sprawled in disarray and arms flung wide. I could see where her blood was caking the ground.

"The ground must have been very dry," I remember thinking, since the blood didn't appear to spread, but rather soaked right into the dirt.

I knew there had to have been a lot of it. My hand reached down to feel the warmth, but it was cold. I touched mom's blood looking for some kind of a connection and my hand tingled. I wanted to throw up, but I didn't.

I closed my eyes and once again heard the screaming mass of womanhood. This death, they seemed to say, belongs to all of us.

I began to walk, there on the farm. "The trees are bare, but the lilac trees are flowering", I thought.

It was a warm Michigan day in May, and there were bright yellow buds on the bushes. Unconsciously I inhaled deeply, and felt the calming effect of clean scented air. The odor of alfalfa and horse manure blasted my senses, and medicated me with cherished childhood memories . . . and I thought, "I will survive this day too."

I felt insulated from the world and a little numb. There was a filter between me and other people, like a bubble where I could see people laughing and crying, but it did not touch me.

During this time a person almost has the feeling of being crazy. Screaming would have been a natural response, but hearing the screaming in your mind could be diagnosed as paranoia or some other axis from the DSM IV TR—Diagnostic and statistical manual of mental disorders. (Mental health practitioners often consider this their bible.) It is very important to note that this feeling of unreality is completely normal when one is the victim of a violent crime. Equally as important to note is that each person will deal with the stress in a different and personal way. There is no normal! In my opinion, all five of the Pittmann siblings reacted differently—extroverts became introverts, introverts became extroverts, and my brother became even more introverted. Almost all victims seem to be protected by a feeling of numbness or unreality. This is truly a blessing and with the caring help of family or professionals, allows one to make it through some of the toughest moments.

This feeling can come and go depending on the person and what is currently happening in their lives. It is systematic with shock, but when you are dealing with murder it seems to reappear throughout the cycles of grief. This is an example of why I believe people who are victims of violent crimes have symptoms of PTSD. In "normal" grief— if there is such a thing—this feeling would not be so intense and would not reoccur throughout a person's life time. Please note that I also believe it can reoccur even after a person has come to terms with their loss. In other words, I think a person can be thrown into PTSD when other unrelated traumatic events occur throughout the rest of the victim's lifetime.

"Space for your personal thoughts"

Chapter 3

COPING

Everyone is bickering, wanting a say so in this and that. Linda wanted mom's diamond ring. Sally wanted the ear rings she had on when Brooks shot her. Cindy sat on the sofa with mom's red boots on. My brother, Richard, is so mad; he is looking for a fight. I can't stand the fighting, I'm thinking. Mom is dead.

Yet we gather together to make the tough decisions. Soon we were off to make funeral arrangements. We picked out an exquisite marbled casket for her, that we thought we could afford. We hired a limousine to take us to the burial. Somehow we bought the flowers. Decisions were made with little contribution from me. During the funeral I felt too deeply to fulfill my role as family leader. From that day, I never again thought of myself as the family leader. I was confused by the change in our family dynamics, and didn't recognize my role as it emerged.

Everyone was acting different and all of us were taking on different roles. I was hyper sensitive to everyone's feelings and it made me uncomfortable. We were all so angry, so sad, so everything. The funeral director seemed to me a bully. "Do this, do that . . . you must make a decision," I think he said. I quit paying attention.

Then it was time to go over the pictures we wanted to display. Several bottles of wine later, we had gathered what we needed. I lost time again.

I became the mediator, as I couldn't stand any negative energy around me. I hated the feelings I felt surrounding us and the old farm house, and worked continuously to try to dispel it. I even had a physic come in and bless the house. We said the "Our Father" prayer over every doorway and opening. It sounds crazy now, but I couldn't have stayed in the house without that woman coming out. I think maybe I was a little crazy then.

I was elected by the family to close the estate, so I went home to Houston Texas, packed up my three little ones, came back to Detroit and got to work.
Those summer months were hard. Everyone tried to get something from the estate. People were mean and hateful. I guess the thought of losing money superseded any humane thoughts they might have had towards a

bereaved family member. I dreaded the phone ringing, yet as a form of self-punishment—I guess because I was alive and mom wasn't—I continuously answered its summons.

"She was murdered, she was murdered, she was murdered," I repeated so often it seemed an echo.

"Oh," was the comeback, "well I need . . . ." For me it was so momentous, so huge; yet for creditors and others it was a mere blip in the screen of their lives.

It's funny, but I don't think our family dynamics were ever the same after that. Each of us changed in a very significant way, which in turn affected our family roles. Something like this plays on your weaknesses and strengths, and it is a toss-up how each of the victims will emerge. I became more thoughtful and caring, less self-centered and extroverted. I imagine the years ahead will bring back some of my extroversion tendencies, but I will never be as outgoing as I use to be—I find I would rather listen than talk these days.

This is the point where you put one foot in front of the other and get things done. I don't know how things get done, they just do. I paid bills, answered telephone calls, cancelled subscriptions, cleaned out closets, and dealt with greedy relatives. I fed the horses, cleaned the house, met with lawyers, and went through files. I even found out about unspeakable secrets. which remain unspoken to this day. If you asked me to articulate it, I don't think I could. I just went on and did what needed to be done. This is what I believe got me through without going crazy; not really thinking— just doing.

Years later, when 9/11 happened, I fell into another deep depression, much like when my mother died. This time I eventually went for professional help. It took two years to begin to feel some sense of normalcy the first time, and I knew I couldn't afford to lose any more years to grief.

I remember the day it happened, I was a counselor at a middle school and there were things to be done. I answered phones from worried parents; I wrote a statement for the teachers to read to their classes, I did the assembly for the students and teachers.

My Principal, Becky, asked me; "How do you function?"

And I remember saying, "you just put one foot in front of the other and go on . . ."

I had been here before.

When you're depressed you don't feel like breathing let alone moving, so our coping starts with very small steps—talking with friends and family, trying to walk around the block, just doing your routine non-thinking everyday activities.

It helps to develop habits that help you feel better.

A) If you are a nature lover take walks
B) Watch funny movies
C) Avoid the news (life will go on, but you can't afford to hear about it right now.)
D) If you have pets, play with them
E) Music lovers should saturate themselves with their preferred genre
F) Take long hot baths with candles and music
G) Write—no one has to read it and it's a great way of writing away the horrors
H) This is a great time to pick up a new hobby; such as, art, mountain climbing, yoga
I) Study something new—I studied aroma therapy and touch healing (Reiki)
J) Keep yourself healthy:

- Aim for 8 hours of sleep. (When we are depressed we tend towards too much—occasionally too little.)

- Drink plenty of water
- Learn to meditate or pray daily
- Learn relaxation techniques
- Expose yourself to sunlight every day. Did you know that the lack of sunlight can make depression worse?
- Eat healthy
- Take your vitamins—especially B. Deficiencies in B vitamins such as folic acid and B-12 can trigger depression.

"Space for your personal thoughts"

Chapter 4

KNOWING AND DESPAIR

A cloud of unreality protected me as I drove through the back alleys of downtown Detroit, looking for the rental houses my mother and her friend and partner Christine owned—most of which I found were in the slums of Detroit. I was thirty four years old at the time, and this mission turned out to be just a little bit little scary.

Still I thought, "They were working to make the place a little more livable."

A woman tenant came from one of the houses and headed straight for me. She was a tall emancipated woman whose black face was streaked with red welts, and her right eye was swollen shut and seeping yellow ooze. I could tell she was a drug addict. Her ragged clothes did not button and she clutched her shirt closed with one hand. Her feet were so swollen and lacerated; I wondered how she even walked on them. She was determined to make it to me, so I knew she had something important to say. I held out my hand and touched her arm when she reached me, and consciously tried to focus on her good eye.

"Your mom," she said, "cared about people. She always treated me good."

Her eye was damp with emotion as she spoke to me and I was touched. I looked at this woman and knew my mom had felt her pain. My sadness deepened, hopelessness invaded my senses. I had found another person my mom had been trying to help.

"Why did this happen to my mom? She did so much for others", I thought.

I did not think I could go through any more. Where would I get the strength to carry on?

My three year old twins and five year old daughter got the chicken pox that day. It was a miracle. I think if I didn't have that to concentrate on I would have gone crazy. Suddenly, my focus was on my little ones. It was popsicles, oatmeal baths, and more popsicles. I discovered I could get through the day if I took it minute by minute. This I did every day for the weeks and months that followed.

I still kept losing time though. One day at work when I was at lunch, I remember slowly becoming aware that I held my fork in the air with food on it. I must have been taking a bite to eat when I zonked out. When I came to, everyone was staring at me. I still don't know how long I was out like that. Times like these were scary. Those weeks were hard for me. It didn't really matter how busy I kept myself.

There comes a time when you finally get it. There is no going back. No pretending that tomorrow will be different and your loved one will return. It is hard to qualify this feeling with words. The pain is so bad that you literally feel it physically. I cried so much I got sick of myself, but still I cried more. My chest hurt so badly.

I remember thinking, "So this is what a broken heart feels like."

Now, even today, when I hear a song about someone's broken heart, I want to cry. I can remember what it feels like. Country music makes me sad, so I tend to stay away from it.

There are glimpses of normalcy mixed in with the pain. At this point in your grief it is best to stay busy. Routine will give you time to leave your grief behind and your mind some rest. I recommend returning to work. The first day will be the most difficult and it will be challenging to make it through the day. After that there will be moments where you will find yourself hiding in the bathroom or behind some closed door for a few minutes of privacy. These times get fewer and farther between as time passes. Remember, whatever happens—it is normal!

It is okay to cry, rant, or be quiet when others are around. You will be amazed at the capacity of your colleagues' empathy. Those afraid of tears will miraculously disappear. Sometimes they will even find someone to check on you, after their disappearance.

If you work at home, make sure you begin your daily routines. Make play dates for your children or say yes when invited to lunch or dinner. The important message is . . . try not to become over isolated.

It was during this time that I wrote the poem called:

I WONDER

I wonder if you know
The pain that exist within my soul
The feelings of depth too intense to remember
Harbingers of death—bringing no answer

I wonder if you can tell
My loss of innocence
At such an early age
Days remaining blank—an empty page

I wonder if you can see
Floating images that move in the night
Bringing forth unimaginable fear
Sometimes more creepy through my tears

I wonder if you know
The horror I experienced flow
When the womb that gave me life
Was murdered with heavy strife

I wonder if you can appreciate
The bitter irony of my fate
That allowed me to celebrate
In the mist of all that hate

I wonder if she screamed
When the bullets hit her flesh
Did her beautiful eyes still gleam
While awaiting her last breath

I wonder if you can tell
When you look at me
The days I spent enduring Life
While at night exploring Hell

I wonder how I sensed
The umbilical cord being wrenched
Our life connection until her death
Two souls that will be forever enmeshed

I wonder if you can believe
When you look into my eyes
My silent struggle to see
The goodness in you—and in me.

"Space for your personal thoughts"

Chapter 5

FEAR

At night I found myself lying in bed, wide awake, imagining the pain and devastation my mother felt while she was shot, over and over again.

When I did sleep, I had reoccurring nightmares about James Brooks, my mother's murderer, chasing me around the farm house trying to kill me. I would run and hide and he would find me. He would be shooting and reloading and shooting again, while I would dodge the bullets.

I woke up one time and thought I saw three figures in the room with me. They were in shrouds that covered them from head to foot and were just staring at me. They looked evil and I thought they were somehow connected to the devil. It scared me to death. I swear I could really see them, but it must have been some kind of hallucination. I felt afraid for a long time after that; especially afraid of the dark.

For months I had trouble breathing and my heart hurt really badly. I went to the doctors for a checkup knowing that something was really wrong with my heart. It turned out to be severe anxiety attacks and he suggested counseling.

"I am a counselor," I remember thinking.

I really didn't want to talk about what happened to anyone outside my family. Most times I couldn't even bring myself to say what happened out loud. Yet my sisters, brother, and I would spend hours on the phone talking and helping each other through our daily struggles. I don't think I would have made it without them. They were and still are my counselors and best friends.

I firmly believe, however, that a trained grief counselor could have helped so much. I let my pain keep me from this type of individual help. I should have known better. With my second episode of depression—after 911—I practically ran to a psychiatrist. I can't tell you benefits. Along with his very personal counseling, he put me on a low dose of Prozac, which I continue to take even today.

I am fortune my family is filled with those in the helping professions. (Maybe, that is why we survived on our own the first time.) When dealing with murder, however, this might not be enough. Often a professional outside the family will have a clearer perspective. They will most certainly individualize your healing.

Support groups are very powerful and I wish I had taken advantage of this too. Unfortunately, the first group I tried was not a good fit and I never tried again. As a counselor, I have seen the personal growth and relational support that the correct group can provide. Murder and other violent deaths are very different and bring their own set of issues. I believe it is more beneficial to find others who are going through something similar to you. My first personal experience with a support group was advertised as a grief group. I thought that was appropriate. There were people there who were going through divorce and others who recently lost their spouse. While it was easy to empathize with their pain, I didn't feel a connection. I think I should have tried to find a group that included other victims of serious crimes.

Whatever you decide to do, please remember to get help when you need it!

"Space for your personal thoughts"

Chapter 6

LOOKING FOR ESCAPE

As a teacher and mother of 3 children under the age of 5, I stayed pretty busy during the day, but by 8:00 pm they were tucked in bed, and my mind went to work. It was then that I returned to my dark place. I tried to drown my thoughts in a six pack of beer. It didn't work. It seemed the more I drank, the more focused I became. Trying to clear my mind, I found myself drinking more and more. Eventually, I was getting a twelve pack at the supermarket nightly. I became a functioning alcoholic. This was my dirty little secret.

I found out later that many people knew I might be developing a problem. Yet no one had the heart to say anything to me. It's ironic that it was around this time when I went for training on recognizing and helping alcoholics. This seems to happen a lot in my life—I call them God's little jolts. Fortunately, I recognized myself in this training, and was able to stop my excessive drinking on my own.

I am an avid reader, so I tried to concentrate on reading books. I would finish an entire chapter and then couldn't remember a sentence of what I just read. I would read a chapter over and over again trying unsuccessfully to concentrate. These were moments, however, when I could lose myself. This was a moment when my mind could rest.

Ultimately, I would be left staring into the darkness once again. There really was no escape.

What I have discovered is that there is no escape from the pain a violent crime can create within a person. There is no easy path. When we accept this, and move through the pain, healing can begin. It hurts, I know, but you will be a stronger, wiser, more vibrant person at the end of this journey. Your capacity for loving will increase tenfold, if you let it. Your eyes will be opened to the pain others endure, and you may be able to help ease that pain.

One day, in an old country Tennessee church, sitting next to my Uncle Duke, I wrote this poem. It seems to fit in this chapter.

PAIN

As he reaches his ugly twisted branches out to me

Grabbing, stabbing, and poking at me

I feel each jagged thrust, each surprising little twist

I truly know my heavy heart

As I observe the band around my chest

I can feel it getting tighter and tighter

And when my legs fold beneath me

Too soon—too often—the floodgates open

And my tears begin to flow

I accept the wetness and feel the cleansing

Facing my pain—experiencing it

And when I can no longer bear my thoughts

I'll take a deep breath and walk through my invisible walls

Only then will I be able to see the beauty in those knotted branches

For I have come to understand

As an observer of life, and an active participant

The happiest people in this world

Are the ones who have known deep sorrow.

"Space for your personal thoughts"

Chapter 7

SLIPPERY SLOPES

My sister, Cindy, practiced yoga and suggested I take it up. Both the spiritual aspects and the exercises helped me to become more in touch with my body. The meditation was extremely hard for me to master, but I had a great teacher. I kept after it and eventually I was able to quiet my mind. It was such a relief to be quiet and not think of anything!

In spite of this, one night I started thinking about killing myself. I would think things like, "my car could just crash into that tree while I'm driving. It wouldn't be my fault then. I just wanted to die. I wanted the pain in my heart to go away, but with three small children under the age of five, I knew I had to fight it.

I was in trouble and had to get my mind right, so I began to do what I always did during times of stress.

I began to write furiously. Just to clear my head and gather my thoughts. I wrote poems about my pain and disillusionment. I wrote about the abuse that shaped my mother's life and how she turned it into her strength. I wrote letters to my friends and family sharing my pain. In a series of poems written by me, I called myself **she** *because at that point it still couldn't be* **me**. *I had to separate her; the one who went through the tragedy, from me; the one who still functioned every day.*

It was still too painful.

SHE WHO IS ME

She is walking

Now she is running

There is pain ahead of her

Of this she is sure

Is she crying?

She does not know

She is falling

But there is no floor

She is crawling

Trying to find her way

Back into the womb

But it is dead

"Space for your personal thoughts"

SHE WHO IS ME

She is running

Her feet land softly above the ground

Her thoughts are full of fantasy

Romance and adventure

Fictitious characters all

She avoids her deeper thoughts

Instead exists outside

After fifteen years of studying

She finally understands

The author—Sylvia Plath

And she patiently awaits

Her own glass bell.

"Space for your personal thoughts"

I think at this point it is very important to begin learning new things. I suggest Julia Cameron's book called, *The Artist Way,* to help lead you in the right direction. Julia believes in writing every morning to clear out the garbage in the mind. Then you can begin to experience your day. By completing this book you will challenge yourself and find creativity you never knew you had. I have actually worked through this book twice with several years in between. That is how powerful I think it is for self-healing and self-growth.

However, there are many self-help techniques you can learn that may be more in tune with your personality. There is a workshop I present to a variety of audiences called "Wellness-Keep Calm and Carry On." I would like to share a brief synopsis of the presentation, as I believe it could be useful to you.

My training topics include:

Stress—the good, the bad, the ugly

Recognizing the benefits and dangers of stress will help you pin point what is happening in your own body.

STRESS {THE GOOD}

- Gets you up and Moving
- Without any stress at all our lives would be boring and pointless
- Some of us need the motivation

STRESS {THE BAD}

- It *WILL* destroy your mental and physical health
- Blood Pressure Rises
- Breathing Becomes More Rapid
- Digestive system slows down
- Muscles become tense
- Lack of Sleep

STRESS {THE UGLY}

- High Blood Pressure
- Weight Gain/Loss
- Pinched Nerves/Muscles
- Loss of Hair
- Unable to fight off viruses
- Fatigue
- Personality Changes

THE POWER OF POSITIVE THINKING

During my years of counseling, I have been privileged to hear many personal and tragic stories. One thing I now know is . . . everyone has a story.

- Sometimes life sucks
- How it effects each of us is a matter of Choice—Your Choice.
- Every day we can make a choice to have a good day or bad day.
- It really is that simple.

THE VOICE

Most of us inherit or learn to use a negative voice inside of our heads. We have to work to quiet their babbles. There are four main voices—do you recognize yourself?

- The Worrier
- The Perfectionist
- The Critic
- The Victim

BRAIN REFRAMING

Once you recognize your voice, you can change those negative internal dialogues and replace them with positive counter statements.

- Practice
- Partner Up to help each other reframe
- Pay attention to your thoughts

LAUGHTER

Have you ever been to a funeral where you see family members laughing? It happens because people innately know about its healing power. History, traditions, and experience all teach us that humor has great health value.

Physical Benefits of Laughter

- Boosts immunity
- Lowers Stress Hormones
- Decreases Pain
- Replaces Your Muscles
- Prevents Heart Disease

Mental Health Benefits of Laughter

- Adds joy and zest to life
- Eases anxiety and fear
- Relieves Stress
- Improves Mood
- Enhances Resilience

Social Benefits of Laughter

- Strengthens Relationships
- Attracts others to us
- Enhances Teamwork
- Helps Defuse Conflict
- Promotes Group Bonding

WRITING TRASH

With this technique you write your morning thoughts continuously in a journal for 20 minutes without stopping. Julia Cameron calls this her Morning Pages. Are you upset about something? Do you feel Irritable? Is something great happening right now? Do you feel sluggish?

- Be honest and clarity will come
- Maybe you need to make amends with someone
- Perhaps you need some time for yourself
- Maybe it is just time to take out the trash for the garbage people to pick up!
- Note to self—some garbage doesn't need to be left around for others to read. (Throw it out or burn it in a ritual to release your feelings!)

BIO FEEDBACK

This technique helps people become aware of how their bodies and thoughts feel when stressors are occurring. Some techniques can be very intense while others are more fun and less invasive.

- Thermal biofeedback measures skin temperature. Electrodes are attached to the skin and this feeds information to a monitor. A client can then learn to recognize their stressors and recondition their reactions.
- [I use Bio Dots in my workshops as a fun, cheap, somewhat accurate method

of relaxation that you place in the crease between your thumb and fore finger. Colors are related to the temperature of your hands. The theory is the warmer your hands the more relaxed and stress-free a person feels. So you can think your hands warm!]

- Electromyography measures muscle tension. Therapist can read the information and through trial and error single out mental activities that will help individuals regulate their body processes. This can be very informative to someone who has tried multiple techniques and met with failure.
- Neurofeedback measures brain wave activity. I talk a lot about this in my workshop while discussing hypnotherapy.

All of these types can be cost prohibitive if your insurance does not recognize the health benefits. But is a good choice over drugs because of its noninvasive qualities and the fact that it has no side effects.

YOGA

This is by far the best exercise I have found for myself. In my workshop, I teach Tadasana (Mountain Pose). This pose can be used while waiting in line, at the airport, or anytime you find yourself just waiting. I recommend you find a teacher, so that you learn the correct forms and techniques to receive its full benefits.

HYPNOSIS

There are three types of hypnosis: hypnosis with a practitioner, ITunes-CD's-Tapes, and self-hypnosis. What most people don't realize is that all hypnosis is 100% voluntary; therefore, all hypnosis is self-hypnosis. It cannot happen without your cooperation. Although, I will admit, some minds are easier than others to hypnotize. When entertainment is the goal, the hypnotist is looking for those types of people in the audience. (They use subtle tests when they are talking to choose their participants.)

The more relaxed a person becomes, the more susceptible they are to suggestion or hypnosis. Our brain waves actually decrease which puts us in the perfect condition to receive suggestions.

Brain Waves Graph

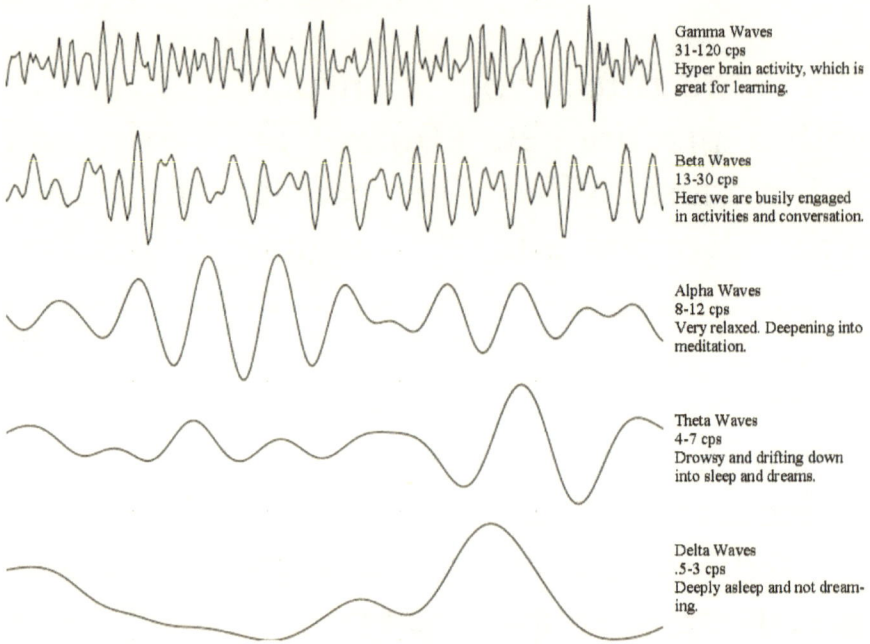

Gamma Waves
31-120 cps
Hyper brain activity, which is
great for learning.

Beta Waves
13-30 cps
Here we are busily engaged
in activities and conversation.

Alpha Waves
8-12 cps
Very relaxed. Deepening into
meditation.

Theta Waves
4-7 cps
Drowsy and drifting down
into sleep and dreams.

Delta Waves
.5-3 cps
Deeply asleep and not dream-
ing.

Gamma brain waves have the highest frequency at 25 to100 pulses. Research has shown this level of functioning is optimum for learning and creativity. Studies show that test scores have improved using music that uses these frequencies. The music causes our brainwaves to equal the higher pulse rate.

Beta is emitted when we are consciously alert, or we feel agitated, tense, or afraid. This can be measured with frequencies ranging from 13 to 60 pulses per second in the Hertz scale. This is how most of us function throughout our days.

Alpha is when we are in a state of physical and mental relaxation, although we are aware of what is happening around us, its frequency are around 7 to 13 pulses per second. This is the perfect state for hypnosis.

Theta is indicated when more or less 4 to 7 pulses are measured. It is a state of somnolence with reduced consciousness. One way that I can tell a client is in the theta range is when they begin lightly snoring. This state is highly effective when teaching new habits or getting information that has been locked away.

Delta happens when there is unconsciousness, deep sleep or catalepsy, emitting between 0.1 and 4 cycles per second. I believe recordings or tapes are extremely powerful during this time. This is why I hate for people to sleep with the television turned on. Our minds will take in anything and everything. Have you ever noticed the amount of food commercials that are aired in the evening? This is a very successful marketing tool for them. Pay attention to your first thoughts of the day if you run the television when you sleep.

It has been my experience that this technique is extremely powerful when navigating the field of grief. The quickest way to experience this is with a trained therapist. My training took two intense weekends a month for two years. Be careful of the charlatans claiming to be a hypnotherapist—quite often it is a ploy to sell expensive vitamins. Ask about their history before you employ them.

I would also caution you to find someone with counseling experience. You will need someone to help guide you through your intense emotions. Health practitioners are trained to help you navigate your grief.

Remember, you must be a willing participant who completely trusts your therapist for the session(s) to be successful. Without trust your sessions will not be successful. This is why taking time to build rapport with your therapist is so useful.

Most importantly, be comfortable in the knowledge that it is nearly impossible to make someone do something that goes against your core values. This would require far more time, techniques, and skill than a hypnotherapist would know.

"Space for your personal thoughts"

Chapter 8

MAKING SENSE OF
THE BAD TIMES

The murder trial was in January. This was eight months after the murder that had occurred in May. It was pretty bad. I tried to feel hatred toward James Brooks, the man who killed my mother, because I thought that was what I was supposed to feel. Instead, I just felt an overwhelming sense of sadness and grief. Most of the time, however, my emotions were on hold. As I sat in the courtroom that first day waiting for the sheriff to bring him into the courtroom I remember thinking, "I hope I don't faint, I hope I don't faint."

Since we were given the first bench in front of the courtroom, we could see what was happening pretty clearly. I looked at him and searched his face for some kind of remorse. Instead I saw a self-satisfied smirk. I really didn't understand what was going through his mind. Throughout the week of her trial I became devastated when I realized the full extent of my mother's injuries. Four misfired bullets lay at her feet before the fifth bullet successfully discharged from three to four feet away. She must have known what was coming. I wonder what she was thinking of as she waited for what was to follow. At least 8 large pellets and several smaller pellets slammed into her abdomen, and then traveled a path through her liver, intestines, colon, aorta, kidney, stomach, diaphragm, and lung. My heart aches with the images of horror I envision her experiencing at that moment. Did she feel her ring finger being ripped away from a direct birdshot hit? Or did it happen too fast for her to feel anything?

My sisters and I fought to see the police photographs of the crime. My brother wanted no part in seeing them. At first the prosecutor was not going to allow us to see them saying, "There's no reason. It will be too painful."

Yet we persisted, so they relented. We gathered together near the end of the trial right there in the court room.

I remember it was so quiet we could hear each other breathing. Very quietly the courtroom had been cleared. The police and prosecutor stood aside a few feet away from us watching.

It seemed like everyone was watching us all the time—the TV reporters, the jury, the other people in the courtroom.

According to the 911 operator, the photos were taken nine minutes after my mother was killed.

All four of us girls each took time to look at every photo—they were indeed violent. There were even pictures from the pathologist from when she had been autopsied. Those were kind of a shock to me at first, but I was glad to see where every wound was located. My imagination had built the murder to unbelievable proportions, so that those pictures actually brought me some peace.

Most of my friends tried to convince me not to attend the trial. I knew for me it was necessary. I truly believe that most of us need this time to process what happened. We need to hear the testimony of witnesses. We need to look into the juror's eyes. We need to see what kind of clothes and jewelry they wear. One juror wore a medallion of the Lambda symbol, which is a symbol used to promote gay and lesbian rights. This was a comfort to me. These things helped me to trust the jury.

I was able to hear their gasps when they heard my mother's story. I was able to see their scowls, when James Brook's lawyer tried to earn their sympathy by persecuting my mother and her partner. Apparently, they had been flaunting their lifestyle by publically kissing. It was comforting to know that most of the jurors were on our family's side. In our case, there was no doubt of his guilt, but we were hoping for maximum sentencing. I know we evaluated the prosecutor to make sure he was doing a good job. We looked at Brook's lawyer with disbelief and anger. We watched the police as they guarded the prisoner—James Brooks, our neighbor for over 20 years.

There was a group of gay and lesbian activist that came to court every day. They were very respectful of us, and made sure we knew our mother was a beloved part of their community. One evening they held a candle light vigil in downtown Detroit where thousands of people attended. I was shocked and humbled by their support. I thought, "Wow, my mother sure did have a lot of friends."

Later, I found out that mom was very active leader, who pushed for change and acceptance. There is currently a documentary being made about my mother's story and a fictional book that uses her and her partner as characters in the story. Detroit also houses an art museum named in their honor. I think maybe this was the momentum needed at the time to initiate change.

The media was allowed into the courtroom, so there were many pictures of my family in our unguarded moments. One newspaper from the *Detroit News* tried very hard to write an honest and factual report of the proceedings every day. She was very interested in getting to know all five of my mother's children. She was the only honest representative for the media. I wish I could remember her name, so that I could give her credit. For the most part, the media manipulated the truth to find the most sensational twist they could. Some even made up their own facts.

I do think it was somewhat healing for us to talk with the television and radio stations though.

People needed to see, up close and personal, the devastation hate crimes can cause communities.

We ask ourselves why did this happen? What did mom do to cause this? But is that really the important question? Is there ever a good reason for someone to commit murder? Society needs to focus on the criminal—not the victims.

It is always very healing to bring good out of the bad things that happen to us. Many people bring awareness and change through turning their pain into something useful. Think of M.A.D.D—Mothers Against Drunk Drivers. They have been very instrumental in changing our laws and bringing harsher punishment to drunk drivers.

It doesn't have to be a group or committee to make a difference. Sometimes it can be more personal. I have devoted my life to learning how to help others. Sometimes, I teach a class or present a workshop. Mostly, I quietly help one person at a time, and that works for me.

"Space for your personal thoughts"

Chapter 9

THE SEARCH FOR THE TRUTH

When the guilty verdict came in I felt nothing. It wouldn't bring my mother back. Nor would it stop my tears which still seemed to erupt without warning. James Brooks looked stoic and somewhat proud, which pissed me off. He would be living off the state for the rest of his life. Actually, he would be serving a double life sentence with some added years for illegal possession of weapons. I wanted to throw up.

The court bailiff won my heart, when he motioned for the police, pointed toward Brooks, and said, "Come and get this garbage out of here."

He got what I was feeling.

I started thinking then about the death penalty. I had always been adamantly opposed to it, but I really began to question myself. I was angry that it appeared he'd gotten off lightly. A deputy told me afterwards it was really hard on people who have their freedom taken away. I didn't care. I still wanted him dead.

Today, many years later, I am glad he wasn't put to death. I don't really know why. I remember that throughout my teen and early twenties, I actively cried out against the death penalty. At that time, I was heavily involved in political demonstrations, writing my congressman, and— when I turned 18— voting for whatever candidate felt the same way.

Brooks, the man I had enjoyed afternoon coffee with, ended up dying in prison—a bitter unhappy man. But at the time of this journal entry, if you asked me if I believe in the death penalty, I would have to say a conflicted yes. It is not something I like to think about, it just seemed; an eye for an eye kind of thing.

Today there are thirty two states that have the death penalty. Of the eighteen states—nineteen if you include the District of Columbia—who do not allow the death penalty, Michigan was the first to abolish it in 1846. Their reasons for this are solid, and they make a good case for the public's opinion. Notably, there have been juries that might put someone on death row that could be innocent of the crime. Unfortunately, we know this has happened, due to new DNA testing now available. Still, I ask myself, "Why do so many states still maintain the option of giving the death penalty."

The Boston Bar Association currently opposes the use of a Federal Death Penalty stating; "their research confirms that the death penalty prosecutions, including federal death penalty cases, are more expensive and time consuming, more subject to prolonged delays, and unlikely to produce a different result than when the prosecution seeks life without parole." Lofty words for sure, but to me death is definitely a different result than life without parole. That is the dilemma for people like me. There really is no clear answer to questions of this nature.

The former Chief Justice of the California Supreme Court, Ronald George, who has always upheld the death penalty, states his concerns regarding the inequities of its use within the state of California. There was a recent report (2009) by the Death Penalty Information Center that showed 96.6 % of the death sentences came from six of the fifty-eight counties in California. This is a compelling case to show the inequities that exist even within a State. I know life isn't fair, but come on! Murderers choose your county wisely.

There are other issues that have been spouted, but one thing stands out very clearly to me. Why are there so few inmates actually on death row? How often is it really used as a deterrent to crime? In instances like my mothers, where there is no doubt of the murderer, wouldn't the world be a better place without James Brooks in it?

Though, I have always been opposed to the death penalty, when I sat in that court room on that day, I began to have my doubts about right and wrong. Clearly, words and statistics can be twisted to benefit either side of the issue. I guess it boils down to how it affects us as individuals. In my case, I have decided the issue is too big for me and so I leave it in God's hands.

"Space for your personal thoughts"

Chapter 10

ANGER

Sometimes I worry that the pain will block out my memories. I don't want to forget my mom. I want to remember the little things, like the time when she unobtrusively helped a young girl in need. Or when she helped an overstressed mother on her way out of a restaurant button up her five small children's overcoats all the while chattering on about how they would all grow up to be somebody special, just like her five children did.

I want to laugh and remember us burning our bras in a backyard bonfire to show each other that we were firmly supportive of Gloria Steinem and her fight for woman's rights. I want to remember my mom's inner strength and how she never seemed to fit in with the mainstream. I want to remember her signature red cowboy boots. I want to see her proud face encased in a helmet smiling excitedly on top of her Gold Wing Honda.

And, yes, I want to remember the violence of her death, in hopes that the next time I feel like judging someone for being different or doing something that I don't understand I will remember—judging in ignorance breeds hate and hate kills—even generous and warm people like my mom.

Anger is an emotion we are all familiar with and something we have all felt at one time or another. Maybe it was a mild form of anger or full-fledged rage. Generally it is a normal, healthy, and human emotion. People use it to help defend them when attacked.

It is when it rages out of control that problems happen. In retrospect, I can see that James Brooks was an angry man. He was easily frustrated and tended toward much exaggerated and overly dramatic responses to what seemed to me everyday trials and tribulations. He always thought the worst for every situation. There was an incident when we had a neighborhood bonfire that he was angry over something and pulled a gun and shot it. I don't remember what it was about, but we children were taken to the house pretty quickly after that.

Getting control of your anger is perhaps one of the best things you can do for yourself and society. Letting it all out is no longer recognized as a healthy way to express your anger. It does little to help you or the person you're angry with solve the problem. People need to learn ways to control their anger and practice them daily. Like anything else, it won't work unless it has become a habit. Learn relaxation techniques such as deep breathing and relaxing imagery. Later in the book, I will talk more about different techniques that could be used. Just remember the more you practice the better you get.

You also change the way you think. We counselors call this cognitive restructuring. When you're angry you tend to exaggerate and become overly dramatic. Simply change the way you are thinking. Instead of, "Oh it so awful, it can never be fixed, it's terrible," say something like, "I am upset about this, but getting angry won't help me fix it."

Learn the skill of problem solving. Remember that your problem will likely not be solved right away. Use the *"I"* form of communication: "When you _____, *I* feel _____ and *I* want you to _____." This is so simple, but something that works really well.

Probably the best way of controlling your anger is learning patience. I read a Buddhist article on anger management techniques that stated:

> Patience is a mind that is able to accept, fully and happily, whatever occurs. It is much more than just gritting our teeth and putting up with things. Being patient means to welcome wholeheartedly whatever arises, having given up the idea that things should be other than what they are. It is always possible to be patient; there is no situation so bad that it cannot be accepted patiently, with an open, accommodating, and peaceful heart. When patience is present in our mind it is impossible for unhappy thoughts to gain a foothold.

I also looked up some scripture from the bible for us to ponder. I found 101 of them devoted to patience! Here are a few of my favorites:

Romans 12:12

Rejoice in hope, be patient in tribulation, be constant in prayer.

Galatians 6:9

And let us not grow weary of doing good, for in due season we will reap, if we do not give up.

It seems like I have been working all my life on patience. It has probably saved my mind many times. It is so much easier to stay calm and focused on the bigger picture.

"Space for your personal thoughts"

Chapter 11

REMEMBERING THE GOOD TIMES

In time, I begin to think about my mother without that gut wrenching sickness. I could talk about her and remember. There are times when I am sad, but mostly I am telling stories about her escapades to my children. It is the only way they will ever know her. She was definitely worth knowing.

I did take the time to go through my pictures, so that I could preserve them for the future. This process is yet another cleansing ritual that helped me through my grief even as it purified.

During this time, I wrote the ending to my SHE poems. I am sharing this with you for my final page in this very short yet important chapter.

Life is never the same, but you can find a new way to navigate through the next part of it.

I did.

SHE WHO IS ME

Is she alone?

She lifts her head

She sees the birds

Flying high

*Soaring with the Spirits
Together*

There is Pain

But Sometimes

She smells the newly cut grass

The flowers in bloom

She hears the children laughing

Pamala Messinger

The dogs barking

She can feel the beauty

In her heart

Maybe

She will survive.

Final Words

Throughout my career in education, I have taken out my journal many times to read my thoughts about this horrific crime. As difficult as this time period was to get through, I believe my personal experience has made me a better counselor and person. Occasionally I toyed with the idea of creating a self-help book using my experiences, but would decide the timing wasn't right. I would ask myself if I was brave enough to share all of my secrets with the public.

Recently, I have been personally involved with others who are going through the process of surviving a loved one's murder. Suddenly, I knew that the time to publish was now.

Hopefully, I have referenced any direct quotes that I used. I read at least 2-5 books a week, so the lines between what I know and what I have read, sometimes become blurry.

I hope and pray that my words will help in some small way.

May God bless every one of you.

Pamala

References

Cameron, Julia. (1992). The Artist's Way: A Spiritual Path to Higher Creativity, G.P. Putnam's Sons

Cress, Richard, W. (2005). The Value of a Smile: Victimization

101. Book Surge, LLC.

Diagnostic and Statistical Manual DSM-IV-TR. (2000). American Psychiatric Association. Arlington, VA.

Kubler-Ross, Elisabeth. Death, The Final Stage Of Growth, 1975
Prentice-Hall Incorporated.

http://www.deathpenaltyinfo.org

http://www.openbible.info/topics/patience

About the Author

Pamala Pittmann Messinger holds a Bachelor's of Science in Education and a Master's of Science in Counseling. She is a 30 year veteran of the public education system in Texas. Twenty of those years have been spent as Counselor, Mentor, and District Counseling Supervisor. Though the story is placed in Detroit Michigan, Pamala now happily resides in Houston Texas.